Saying It With Flowers

Peter Phillips

Dear Terry,
I thought you'd like to see my latest.
I do hope you are both well.
Warm wishes, Peter.
Do you think you fancy reviewing it for Suburb News?
(I'm at: pcphillipslondon@hotmail.co.uk)
50 Asmuns Hill
NW11 6EU

Ward Wood Publishing
www.wardwoodpublishing.co.uk

Published by Ward Wood Publishing
6 The Drive
Golders Green
London NW11 9SR
www.wardwoodpublishing.co.uk

The right of Peter Phillips to be identified as author of this work has been asserted by him in accordance with the Copyright, Designs and Patent Act, 1988.
Copyright © 2022 Peter Phillips
ISBN: 978-1-908742-75-9:

British Library Cataloguing in Publication Data. A CIP record for this book can be obtained from the British Library.

All rights reserved. No part of this publication may be reproduced, stored in a retrieval system, or transmitted in any form or by any means, electronic, mechanical, photocopying, recording or otherwise without the prior written permission of the publishers. This book may not be lent, hired out, resold or otherwise disposed of by way of trade in any form of binding or cover other than that in which it is published, without the prior consent of the publishers.

Designed and typeset in Palatino Linotype by
Ward Wood Publishing
Cover design by Ward Wood Publishing

Cover Painting:
Parents, Child and Unborn by Simon Turvey
info@mallgalleries.com – Simon Turvey

Printed and bound in Great Britain by
Imprint Digital, Seychelles Farm,
Upton Pyne, Exeter, Devon EX5 5HY

Acknowledgements

Some of these poems, or versions of them, first appeared in: *Acumen, Brittle Star, Genius Floored* (Soaring Penguin), *London Grip, On the Hill, Orbis International, Peace News, Sofia, South Bank Poetry, The Frogmore Papers, The High Window, Uncompassed* (Salmon Poetry).

'Hyacinth' was inspired by a translation by Dinah Livingstone of Lorca's poem 'The Unfaithful Wife'. 'Red Carnations' was selected by Alison Chisholm for a workshop feature in *Writing Magazine* (July 2015). 'Knotweed' was commended in The Barnet Open Poetry Competition, 2015, and appeared in the celebratory anthology. The three poems from 'Geese' were published in the programme: *Songs of Exile and Love*, a recital of music and song, held at St Peter's Church, Hammersmith (November 2019).

Several poems were previously published before appearing in bilingual English/Romanian collections: *Six British Poets*, published by Editura Integral and Contemporary Literature Press (CLP) (2016 and 2017) and *Five British Poets* published by Editura Muzeul Literatui and CLP (2018). These publications arose from collaborations between *poetry pf* and the University of Bucharest, and, amongst others, The Romanian Cultural Institute and The British Council.

In September 2016 Hearing Eye published a pamphlet of four poems with lino cuts by the printmaker Emily Johns. These poems were set to music by the composer David Loxley-Blount. His composition *DuoSet* was performed as part of four lunchtime concerts at St Laurence Jewry, Guildhall Yard in the City of London in October 2016.

The essay 'Inspiration, or where I find my ideas' was published in *Acumen* (99) in January 2021.

I would like specially to thank Adele Ward and Mike Wood for publishing this collection amid all sorts of pressures caused by the pandemic. I also thank Jenny Johnson for comments after kindly reading through the manuscript.

CONTENTS

Saying It With Flowers

Snowdrops	9
Bindweed to the Hedge	10
Bluebells	11
Daffodils	12
Daisy to the Red Rose	13
Wisteria	14
Forget-Me-Nots	15
Three Poems in Memory of Linda Phillips:	
1. *Treasure Hunt*	16
2. *Red Carnations*	17
3. *Iris*	18
Love in Idleness:	
1. *Orchid*	19
2. *Looking for Samphire*	20
3. *Mistletoe*	21
4. *Hibiscus*	22
5. *Crocuses*	23
6. *Magnolia*	24
7. *Blackberry Eating*	25
Hyacinth	26
Peony to Poppy	27
Ukraine Sunflower	28
Wild Flowers	29
Knotweed	30
Buttercup	31
Tulips	32
Poppy Parade	33
Amaryllis	34
Gladioli	35
Cactus	36
Ash Dieback	37
Hollyhocks	38

Blossom:
    Cherry Blossom   39
    Apple Blossom   40
Weeping Willow   41
A Bunch of Flowers   42

Nature Watch

Swan   43
Heron   44
Geese:
    We are all Wild Geese   45
    Geese in Flight   46
    Migrant Goose   46
An Owl   47
Parakeet   48
The Philosophical Pig   49
Conjuror Hare   51
Donkey Ride   54
Command Performance   55
Goldfish   56
Out of the Waves   57
Cloud   58
Plum Brandy   59

Climate Watch

To the Doubters   60
A Fuchsia Flowers in Winter   61
The Sun   62
Flooded McDonald's   64
Heat Wave   65

Inspiration: An Essay   71

About The Author   74

*In memory of Linda Phillips
and for my family*

Saying It With Flowers

Snowdrops

I know we look sad; unfortunately it's instinct.
If your ancestors had seen what we endured,
maybe you'd understand. We were always attracted
to sacred places, holy ground's never-ending peace,
only the sound of bells, the chantings and sheep.

They were on horseback, thundered through the fields
and forests where we lay, some dormant, others in bloom.
The noise… hooves ripped the earth,
then came the cries. It happened all over, but in the east –
Walsingham, Framlingham, swathes of us were

wiped out, others so shocked they didn't see daylight
for years. We don't like being thought of as sad.
They hadn't come for us but it was a bloodbath,
we were part of it. No, talking doesn't help.

Bindweed to the Hedge

You say we've got a forceful nature.
You're wrong, it's anxiety, that genetic
hand-me-down, internal frown, which like

a poet's passion, has become a habit.
So when we feel it coming on, we twirl around

your roots, climb from ground's dark scrub
till we reach the top, open our trumpet flower,
breathe out, relax in daylight. We've tried

meditation, mysticism, nothing too controversial,
that kind of spiritual thing doesn't work. Chatting

with a dog rose is helpful, smell of Norfolk lavender
calming. We don't really want to be any other
kind of weed. But seaweed might be nice,

out on a soothing wave, just floating.

Bluebells

Have you heard us ring?
An incantation, notes scattering
through the forest floor
to make a song.

And what about the words,
where will those come from?

From those you mourn,
their will of love
whose calls are answered
with our song.

Daffodils

Dear House, it wasn't difficult
to fall for you, tall bay windows
letting light, soft as Egyptian
linen, linger everywhere,

and daffodils queueing along
the path to the door, waiting for spring's
warm air. Forty years of Februaries,
two births, the death. Now you belong

to others. How nice, a family
with new twins. Soon daffodils will
bloom. Why did I know the day I left
I'd see the first bud blink its yellow eye

as I passed towards another path?

*

And where was that path? Not far.
The hill had heard my whispered wishes,
the casting of neighbours' spells, potions
and with a magician's flourish…

abracadabra… offered me number fifty
as my home. I opened the gate,
saw more daffodils.
One by the step to the door

winked a yellow eye and I said
"Thank you" and went inside.

Daisy to the Red Rose

Don't you wish you were a daisy? Rejoicing
others' love is hard. Much depends on your

beauty, scent, flowers opening just enough
to lure. And thorns along a slender stem –

is that a sort of body piercing?
Daisies may be more demure, yet lovers

want us too; we're easily strung, like pearls.
I'm happy to be white-petalled with a blob

of sun. Is your life really fun? I'm not making
quarrels, Valentine's Day is special,

but who wants to be a posh glamour girl?

Wisteria

I love the way she –
friendly, well-mannered, slightly
stubborn, and with a liking
for wet ground – gently ascends
to first-floor bedrooms. I'm not sure
about her sense of humour. It's good
she's related to the pea family.
I like peas.

She's a blue shade of purple,
you'd recognise her creeping up your wall.
Of course I've fallen for her.
I'd never say anything, wouldn't want
to frighten her off. She likes my brickwork –
my pointing's in good condition.
It wouldn't do to look shabby.

Forget-Me-Nots

"Forget me not" you say, but I can't be sure.
Not anymore. It's the loss of words I notice,
the leaking away of those not so often used.

Of course, if the doctor asks, I'll know
the Prime Minister's name, who are the Queen's
children. If he taps his watch, I'll tell him the time.
If he points to the fabric inside my jacket,
I'll quickly say it's the lining. I still know
Boris promised to make my life great again
and Vikings came from Scandinavia.
But when I lose words faster, will you always

evoke our first Spring, your rush of pink
petals that lit me up, made me blush?
Will I remember you?

Three Poems In Memory Of Linda Phillips

1. *Treasure Hunt*

It should have been you walking the fields to the jetty
searching for treasure with her:

stone, dandelion, clover.

Our granddaughter reaches for blackberries,
finds a plump one for me:

red reed, buttercup, a piece of wood.

As sun falls into the water
we watch the tide sweep the river inland.

The cooling air is warmed by her chatter.

I find a crab shell and samphire;
she puts them in her box.

Forty-one was much too young.

2. Red Carnations

If only I could say let's meet at St Pancras,
not below the android-looking couple clinching
under the clock, but next to Betjeman's statue,
crumpled, loveable, human.

You haven't seen the station, done-up
in all its magnificence; that long, glitzy
champagne and oyster bar at the track's edge.
I still don't like oysters and you never tried them.

The first thing I'd do is talk about the children:
daughter as good as her word
never working for big business, our son
becoming an arts writer. I know it will never

happen, but if it did, I'd carry a whole
bunch of red carnations, so you couldn't miss me.

3. Iris

Your last few weeks.
Your colour drawing of Iris, signed Linda.
Your wish that you'd been an artist.
Your note, *Don't worry, I think you're terribly handsome.*
Your pollen blown in the air to our children.
Your framed drawing, Iris fading in daylight.

Love in Idleness
(*Seven Poems*)

1. Orchid

Standing tall
and slinky,

it's your uppish
white-wine elegance

the boldness
of knowing

you can wear
the shortest of skirts,

your moonlit lips
I'd love to kiss –

but once
is not enough.

2. *Looking for Samphire*

If you ask *Will you come to the beach?*
I'll say, I prefer to walk the coastal path
and on the way hold your hand, put an arm
around you, kiss your cheeks, your lips,
and I'll start to dissolve. We'll carry on walking,

look for new-season samphire, glistening
on the marsh. Each time we kiss I'll thaw
some more. We'll come to the track leading
towards Blakeney and the *Red Lion*, yes,
I kept quiet about that. A bottle of White will

appear and we'll guzzle it, not because we like it
(although we do) but thankful for what it's doing to us.
And we'll see samphire is being served. I'll ask
for some, piled on toast, then a shared order of chips.
You'll say *That's just what I was thinking*

and I'll ask, What else are you thinking?
You'll say *We've nearly finished the samphire,
it's undone us enough, let's get the bus back.*
And all the time I'll have the film music
to *Local Hero* running through me, and you'll ask,

Where are you? But it'll be too late. I'll have melted.

3. Mistletoe

What a weight of kisses!
So many to carry. And today?
A snatched one between a secretary
and senior partner. Then the office boy
with lady from Human Resources.
He wanted two kisses, so did she. Gosh,
she's asked him back. Who's this?
It's head of Accounts, standing
underneath, helplessly hopeful. I'm

having a busy night. And Me?
You're really interested? I come from
a small village outside Hereford. I think
my small pearl-like berries are more beautiful
than the real thing. For a start, kisses are free –
imagine a world without Mistletoe. What,
you've never been kissed under me?
Go on, find someone. Have a go.
Yes, I'll make sure you'll enjoy it.

Try him. Oh, you prefer her.

4. Hibiscus

He bends forward, slowly kisses
lightly on a flower, moves
to another, more kisses,

then strokes a leaf, a gentle caress
between thumb and forefinger.
Doesn't he know what he's doing?

When he touches a bud it flutters,
bursts open, and I feel as if sun
is rippling through me, the heat

of sap rising, like a flow of lava.
I hope he hears my urgent sighs.

5. Crocuses

Blue and yellow flames
are shooting up like gas lights
burning in the chilly air. I crouch

to warm my hands and as I rise
they blow me kisses.
I feel their heat scatter my face.

I bend towards them, say
Thank you, that was breathtaking,
and they do the same again.

6. Magnolia

This evening you're a Spanish dancer,
flashes of pink on your cheeks –
castanets chattering into the night.

Overcome with your magnificence
I can't help saying:
"How wonderful you look this evening"

and on hearing this for the hundredth time
you still blush, just enough to make me think

what would happen if I pulled a branch
full of you towards me, kissed
your white flesh?

Would your petals shower down,
cover me in your embarrassment?
Or would you say, more please *señor,* more?

7. Blackberry Eating

It was a blackberry and your alluring smile
that made me pluck this bulging fruit.

It was you who kissed the stains from my
mouth with a grin so happy, I reached

for another. *I know your game* you said,
as once again you kissed my face clean.

Was it tempting trouble? Maybe, but just
as I stretched for another blackberry,

looked forward to its explosion in my mouth
and what was to follow – just as I was balancing

on tiptoe, my arm extended towards a fully grown,
almost bursting piece of autumn with a mouthful

of tangy juice – it was you who softly said
If you like kissing, why don't you just ask?

Hyacinth
(After Lorca)

I touch your drowsy
breasts, feel their buds spring open.
My warmed hand tingles.

Peony to Poppy

I'm more sophisticated.
I don't have your wilderness-troubled
spirit in my petals. In a few weeks
they'll be falling,
rubies gleaming on the ground.

*It's true our flowers sag with history,
but your silk scarf world
is not for us. I prefer verges to vases.*

There's no need to take that tone,
peonies are fancier than poppies after all.

*It's not about what we look like,
our red spreads deeper than yours.*

Ukraine Sunflower

Dogs were howling. I don't know what breed
but something like wolves; so maybe Alsatians.
They wouldn't stop, their noise was contagious.
Soon we were all weeping. When they came,

we quietened, but not the dogs. Soldiers picked
through our debris-scorched field. Most wore
balaclavas. Only yesterday, children had skipped
through us, laughing at how tall we were.

We don't feel tall now. Soon trucks arrived,
more soldiers. The dead were found, their
pockets emptied. Dogs kept howling. Pieces
of the plane were scattered, some crushed us.
I said, 'Can we still be called Sunflowers?'

And the dogs? They were shot.

Wild Flowers

They appeared amongst us last year.
Caterpillars won't eat their leaves.
Butterflies won't land on them.

I've only once seen a bee rest on their
stalks. It died, instantly. If you don't
believe me, ask the badgers and bats,

they see what's happening. Ask the crows
and herons. Ask the beetles, crickets,
grass snakes; they hear them rustle

through the undergrowth. All flowers,
especially in the desert, will tell you the same.
Here, they're in our meadows, hedgerows,

forest floors. Their numbers keep growing.
We don't know what to call them,
they're called by different names.

What about Knotweed?

Knotweed

Don't even dream of winning –
    you've read the reports
        seen us on YouTube
    cringed at the images.

You think you can get us
at ground level
breaking through foundations.
Once we're properly out, on the march, that's it, unless
you purge deep.

Our
roots
are
deeper
than
you
can
dig.

We know biological control is under trial.
    You decide if chemicals are ethical.

You want a solution
but there is none.

You won't find us
but we're everywhere
    waiting.

We decide when to strike.
    We're in your garden.

Buttercup

Allo mate, I'm the flower meadow's wide boy,
golden grin shining along the river Rother. Words,

or should I say, seeds, are spreading – I've outsmarted
the big boys. But they won't let a bumpkin like me

into their city dens. I have to be content with fields, grow
my fortune by sleight of petal, scatter funds about:

a brass plate in Northiam, a P.O. box in Peasmarsh,
searching for the holy grail, no purchases or sales, only

a bank account swollen with money. Yes, I might
be grassed up by the marsh lands, my tax haven

in Rye Harbour seized. But I'll smile on the other
side of my cup, blame our financial advisers,

Ragwort, Cowslip & Co. Perhaps they'll be raided.
The Sussex meadows would miss us, they'd have

no flash buttercups to feel self-righteous about.
But you can't stop a geezer like me from flowering –

or should I say blooming, and I don't mean blooming
awful. Yes, I do think their lives would be duller,

but I'd be back. I'm off to Jersey, where I have family
and wild flowers like me are cut a bit of slack on tax.

Tulips

They looked like a field of black tulips.
Truly, this was the image in my head.

Then they started stomping.
Their black boots marched,

iron crosses glittered on their tunics.
I stood, stared as the straight-backed

black patch advanced towards us.
Mother grasped my hand, turned to father

and said, "Come, we're leaving today."

Poppy Parade

I'd seen Jack's guts strewn
like manure, his eyes entreating
that final kindness. I broke his neck,
the snap like a distant rifle shot.

My pinstripe suit stinks from battlefield
sweat. When they march past, I see
Jack's grin, a Player's wedged between
yellow fingers, a pint flushed down
his throat, then pissed against the pub's wall,
the wink before he passes out.

When the parade is over, I stare
at the photo ragged with memories,
replace it in my wallet, unpin the poppy,
let it fall to the ground.

Amaryllis

I'm a big boy. Why be shy?
Some are born with attractive smiles
others get by with charm. And me?
I've told you, I'm endowed.

Christmas is my season; I'm in demand –
£6.99 at your local M&S – less if I'm
on offer. A stocking filler, except I'm more
satisfying than that. At first I grow slowly
in millimetres, and when the lady
of the house touches my stem, I'm praying
Please do that again,

and when she asks her husband,
"Where shall I put it dear?"
I shout in hopeful silence
Next to the Hibiscus and do it quickly.

Gladioli

Yes, I do think toilet humour is undervalued.
I heard it's something to do with finishing school
but I didn't go to one actually. I went
to a florist in Catford. They insisted I attend

for at least six months. My first appearance
was with Dame Edna Everage. Armfuls of glads
were taken on stage then thrown to the audience.
I still love bright lights, the magic.

Sir Les Patterson, the cultural attaché, would
leer at me. He often had his flies undone.
We joked about what he'd look like naked,
whether he had a big one.

He was awfully rude. One day he passed wind
right in front of me. Of course I ignored it,
I'm a good girl, I am.
He just looked straight at my stamens and said,

"Your turn darling, I expect yours smell wonderful."
Dame Edna wouldn't have said that. She may
have passed a slight ripple, said "Sorry possum,
that wasn't me, it was just the curry talking."

That's why we respect her, our relationship
is antibiotic. Have I used the right word?

Cactus

The carer comes up close, looks straight into
my face, asks *How are you today, dear?*

My words, but not my thoughts, are like
a jumble of clothes in a black sack,

but not all the time. If she holds my hand,
stays a little longer, I might answer,

but no one wants to touch me. She edges away.
I share the window-ledge warmth

with the cactus, looking out at the car park,
sniffing unchanged water from the vases.

I need a shave. My face is prickly.
If only my tongue would loosen…

How do I feel? How do you l think I feel?
Oh dear, I shouldn't have snarled at her.

God, if there is one, let me bloom once more.
Allow me to remember to nod if she asks

Do you need changing?

Ash Dieback

We recall stories from the ghettos,
the yellow stars, groups rounded up.

Eastern Europe trembles as leaves fall.
Now we've been identified it spreads

like an advancing army through
acres of forest. They take us all.

Don't talk about hope, they're
determined. Yes, we're terrified,

this is selective. You mention other
parallels. They are never identical,

just a different form.

Hollyhocks

A giggle of skinny schoolgirls, ciggies
hanging from their mouths,
as smoke curls into the 1950s.
They're boarders of course, learning
naughtiness will get them everywhere
as they loiter at the back of the flower beds
by the garden wall, jauntily
mocking the geraniums –
those new girls, who behave,
do their homework on time.

As they bloom taller, grow leggy
their haughty flowers laugh,
boast about the raunchy sex
they had with the bad boys
from next door's garden –
except of course, they didn't.

They look forward to the rave –
their end of year dance,
when they'll pretend their superiority
is bred from Daddy's trade in foreign places,
too hot to enjoy really.
And as the summer term dwindles,
the girls sag in vitality, wave goodbye.
Their pink and purple flowers fade
as the St Trinian's Head Gardener
cuts them down to size.

Blossom

Cherry Blossom

You're an elderly lady's hair-do
    reminiscent of someone
        from another era

who fell through your branches
    of backcombed fluffed-up petals
        and like most young girls

now delights in the colour pink

*

What is the attraction of pink
    does it make you feel feminine
        or is it something inexplicable

like a smile from a lover
    who never seen again
        blows a kiss of long ago memories

and makes you feel less blue

Apple Blossom

A wedding dress smiles so wide
   I can't help but return her smile
      as she showers white petals all around.

A swirl of fizzy fragrance
   moves me to touch
      makes me feel I want to be drenched

in her intricate lacework.
   The breeze blows stronger.
      I become light-headed.

Weeping Willow

All those tears, your life's
sadness, gracefully draping
the edge of despair.

*

Late afternoon sun
does not suppress your sorrow.
I wish you would smile.

*

Green cavern of tears –
who hurt you, who will unlock
the skylark in you?

*

A swan sits beneath
your shade. Her cygnets scramble
towards your sorrow.

*

One day you'll be bored
of weeping. You will have dried
all your tears. What then?

A Bunch of Flowers

Mr White, or can I call you Bob?
I promise you this:
we will take great care of your heart.
The surgeon, yes that's me, from India,
I will lead the operation.
An anaesthetist from Syria
will put you to sleep,
a nurse from Sri Lanka
will pass me medical instruments
and we will not leave any inside you.
A junior doctor from Romania
will neatly sew you up
and a porter called Erik, from Sweden,
will wheel you back.

Does that sound alright?
I think that sounds rather beautiful, Mr Chakrabarti.
Thank you, Bob.
I look forward to hearing your heart beating strongly.

Nature Watch

Swan

Sometimes Thomas imagines gliding on the Thames
cosseted in her feathers, his hands a trail in the water,
then splashing his face with cool palms.

He marvels at the swan's grace.

He loves the river gently turning into summer fields,
cows with destinies engraved on their flanks,
buttercups gleaming on the fringe of the water.

And her dusty cygnets bobbing in the wake's lace.

He thinks of portraying this scene, the restful lull
of creativity many prayers away from his life.
But however much he daydreams, the future

will not be wrapped in a swan drifting under the sun.

Now he imagines the final journey from Chelsea,
his shudder as the barge hits the rickety pier,
an arm offered as he alights, the place of execution.

Heron

A heron lands on the hedge's wide runway,
feathers grey, black flash on wing.

This Grandee stares at the water,
looks for air bubbles pricking the surface,

hopes a fish will edge from the gloom.
But there's no movement to dive at

just a low wind patterning the light's reflection.
He looks up, meets my stare, long bill pointing,

turns his head, dives into the pond,
drowns the lilies as he rummages

for frogs in the darkness. Nothing.
He should have aimed at the sparrow

as she drinks from the pool on the path.
Up flies heron chased by two common crows

caw cawing as he soars, then returns,
wing span flapping. Just one more glance.

Geese

We are all Wild Geese

crossing seas, fields, lowlands, plotting the hypothetical,
to flee homelands, either in our heads, or really doing it.
You say, *It's not my turn. Why should I want to leave?*

Don't worry, the reason will present itself. Except you
can't fly, only flee. But even if you were a Goose, could
flap your wings for hours, days and weeks, taking rest

in grasses and riverbeds, however hard you flap,
scream and shriek overhead, you will find
that geese are not wanted anywhere. The world has had

enough of wild geese. You say, *Where should we go,
is there a place open and could I return?* Just try. Yes,
try for your tomorrows, start over for tomorrow's geese.

Freedom is a good word, but you will realise freedom
depends on your definition.

Geese in Flight

V sign in the sky, arrowhead scudding under
clouds, screeches – a clatter of geese.

Who's leading? Who will fall into the furrowed
fields, hobble towards a leafless hedge to sleep

until the early fox comes for you?

Migrant Goose

Just because I've flown from Egypt to Holland
it doesn't mean I'm Egyptian –
I'm tired and hungry, so please
don't say *Shoo back home*
like you say to the Muslims.

An Owl

white against the dimming Suffolk sky
swoops the river Butley, dives the fields
down into farmland, talons open. She drops

seconds from first sight, a tremor of air,
to clutch a vole running through long grass;
then up again, soars through wet light towards

the barn. A hare crouches, he's crazy from racing,
better safe than risk an owl on the hunt.
Into the barn she flies, feeds shredded vole

to her young, then out to the nearly dark, who-whoing.
Where was that flash of hare? She's not hungry
but wants to hear his shadow criss-cross the meadow,

see the grass quiver with fright.

Parakeet

He perches on the window sill
his green coat sparkling in the sun.

"Hello Boysie," I say. "What do you want?"
He flies over and lands on the garden table.

A glass of red would be nice he squawks.
I pour him grape juice. He drinks it all.

What sort of bird are you? he asks.
I'm a human, not a bird, can't you see

I haven't got any wings? He apologises,
says he feels a little woozy.

Then he soars off, in a large ostentatious loop.
As he passes, he drops a present on my head

and screeches *Thanks for the drink –
and your bald patch.*

The Philosophical Pig

I'm a big porker of a pig – the heaviest
in the pens, fatter than my chum Felix.

The farmer calls me his philosophical pig,
says he knows I pick up what's going on.

I'm a smart pig. I don't like his son,
he's a brute of a boy. If he gets near,

he kicks yer. I'll knock him over,
sit on the oik's head, fart in his face.

I wanted to snout around the yard,
grunt my last gasp on my trotters.

But when the farmer talked of pork chops,
I knew it was time to scoff life's last meal –

potato peelings, mixed with rotted veg.
I breathe in…then again…phwoar, loverly.

I hear the truck. Oh, it's the farmer's runt.
Oi, don't frigging prod me. Drop that fork

or I'll butt you in the plums, grunt, grunt –
bite them off, spit them in the muck and shit.

We're at the killing place. There goes Felix,
poor dear pig… he's shaking. What an exit.

Then a shriek of brakes, loud shout to the oik
"Don't let Pluto go with the others."

I still wince when the farmer calls me that,
doesn't he know the great man's name?

"Get him back in the truck NOW."
I'm a blade's breath from Felix's fate.

I start to feel emotional. I shit where I stand,
no time for any grace. Whew, that's better.

I'll enjoy the ride to the yard. The pink sow
bumps her arse against me.

I don't need asking twice and climb on.
Then I think of Felix, it makes me ache

and I can't get hard. His face is handsome,
drained of colour, the noise – his squealing.

The sow grunts, thoughts of Felix disappear.
Then the truck rattles by. The clatter shifts

my brain to another gear, my urges melt away.
Every time I hear the truck, I feel that sadness,

know I will for ever.

Conjuror Hare

Hare or glimpse of magician, a card sharp, trickster
in a dinner jacket, his top hat askew – speeds
from the field, golden with corn.

His eyes are a nervous twitching. He must be on time,

must find cover, put on a show, an extravaganza,
avoid hawk overhead. He daren't move, daren't
stay still. Decision – mad dash into woods. Whew…

bluff or counter bluff, perfects a few disappearances.

There's clapping, he bows, reappears as himself,
whatever that is. Now you see his cashmere brown coat.
Time for another trick, scatters stars over the children,

wide-eyed, open-eared… WOW, how did hare do that?

Can a hare really do that? His sleight of hand massages
a deck of cards, the wand quivers, blink of eyelashes.
Is he really a hare or magician? Make up your mind.

There's a quietening, the weight of air changes.

He licks his thin lips. Hawk hovers above the forest's roof,
plans angle of flight. Two long seconds, quick decide.
Hare turns afternoon into dusk, hawk is vanished.

Last wave of wand and it's dawn. He steadies his hat.

*

In the field on my side, fragile, nearly a corpse.
That hawk was close, just a hawk's blink away.
I revive, listen to silence, for the tiniest change
of atmosphere, like snow turning to sleet. I feel

I'm losing my senses, worse – powers seeping

away. I fear claws on my shoulders, taking me
as I kick against the air, wriggle to break free.
I hope I'll land on grass, don't break my neck.

A magician told me illusions were his oxygen,

that's now my art. I hope for instant death,
but hope is not enough – I need magic.
Do I still have it? I hold my breath, curl tight,
count to two hundred. My heart almost bursts.

Hawk plunges, but late, a mistimed punchline.

Gone, but where? It's warm, the grass is green.
I'm still The Great Magical Hare
with special powers. Where's my top hat?
I reach for it, place it on my head.

I bow to myself, bound away. I need a drink.

*

But it's old age that worries me.
I polish my sleight of hand,
rehearse till I can do it standing
on my ears. That's difficult
with my long ones. You think

I'm telling untruths! I never do that.
Yes, I can make magic when I sleep.
It's the illusion that matters.
You think I'm a trickster, I'm not.
I'm an artist. Imagine a poet losing

language, playwrights forgetting
how to plot, the wood carver
who drops his tools, philosophers
with tangled thoughts. And remember
I must keep watch for Hawk. He wants

to tear me to mouthfuls. I dread
that death, prefer the dribbling away
of senses. Alright, I'll stop blathering,
go and find lady hare, try the hedges,

plenty of cover there. Where's my top hat?
Oh dear if I lose it I won't be able to think.
I don't want that. Oops it's on my head.
Good, I feel calmed. My head is fizzing,
wizardry is happening.

Donkey Ride

It's your eyes, doleful and kind,
which draw me to you. I climb on your
agéd back, make the usual clicking noise
and we move forward in measured paces.

I'm back, a six-year-old
on Westgate's sand, sea creeping
towards us as we trundle on.
The movement, steady and sleepy

calms my thoughts. I get off, pat your head.
You raise your stare from the beach,
look into my face
as if to say "Thank you."

I don't know why, but I ask
Have you ever been in love?
Of course, there's no reply,
but I can't help saying:

I have twice, and it was worth it.
You seem to understand what hasn't been said
so I pat you again. You trudge up to
the promenade, wait for another ride.

Command Performance

A vixen slopes through the hedge.
I know it's female – she crouches
to piss – then bounds on to the bench.

My breath steams the window. I'm
hushed like a squirrel, not wanting
my stare to alert her. She sits

on her haunches, long back upright
in the spotlight of moon's satin beam,
grey-and-white breast shimmering

like an evening dress. Then she sings,
not the fox shrieks she makes for mating
or calling her cubs, but graduated notes

from a mouth sawtoothed, gleaming
in white light, tongue a rosy pink,
as she, Shirley Bassey of the wild world,

performs her song, thrusts her right paw
in the air as she belts out 'Hey Big Spender'
like she's auditioning for life.

Goldfish

You don't see them at fairs any more
circling around their glass bowl – a prize
for a rifle shot or scooping up a floating duck.

Gone is the plastic bag spilt on the bus home,
the hunt for fish food, the naming ceremony.

Gone is the fish found floating,
our first feeling of loss, tears as Mother
pours Goldy down the toilet.

Gone are our daughters asking why he died –
was he trying to get out, or was he giddy

going round and round? And the answer:
"He was just an old fish, darling."
Then the request for a dog, a small one,

and father says, "If you want a dog you must
walk it, because I'm not." And the final

compromise, to decide whether it's a rabbit,
budgerigar or canary and Father insists
he doesn't care, so long as it's kept in a cage.

Out of the Waves

into the still harbour, my box of fish,
a mixed catch but mainly mackerel,
glistens in the mist. Home soon for a pie,
can already taste its smell,
see the pastry bubble on the oven's shelf.

Pleased the gulls have stopped following,
I trudge up the hill, then leaning on a lamp post,
I hum the tune, fill my pipe.
The chug-chug of the boat fades into Falmouth.

I'm nearly home. The Siamese pads more sprightly
than usual, sashays through my legs,
squeezes under the gate
into the whitewashed cottage.

I think, *You only want me for my fish.*
I enter. The cat picks up my ukulele,
sings my favourite song:
'When I'm Cleaning Windows'.

Cloud

                I'm tired of being a cloud
                        all that darkness
             the tears   anxiety heavy on my
shoulders
                              a pain in your neck
                  a pain in mine
                    just want to blow away
      feel the sun thread through me like a holiday
               yes   even Magaluf will do
       want to stop the grey sideways glances
               the one I've perfected
  to spoil a picnic   a beer on the lawn
         then my routines
              of rain
         suspicion
         sulkiness
               distrust
     of always being talked about
  my gloomy disposition
                    I want to be blown about
happily
   be bright like sparklers on a children's birthday cake
a Victoria Sponge with strawberries and thick cream
              yes
       a lot of it   please

Plum Brandy
(*for Mircea Dinescu*)

Mircea, when I first saw you
your hands were fondling a bottle,
a female bottle, and when

we met again at your restaurant
there she was, the same Romanian beauty,
being gently caressed

as if she were your lover.
When you filled my glass to the top
I drank the shot in one gulp.

It felt like I was kissed on the lips,
in my mouth and then all over.
When you offered me another,

being a polite Englishman
and not yet drunk,
but wanting to behave

I politely declined. But now I wish
I had accepted and had become
completely drunk. So Mircea, I admit it,

I'm smitten, I feel like a jealous lover,
please don't shoot me for declaring this,
have pity but where is the plum brandy?

I'm sure she likes me more than you.

Climate Watch

To the Doubters

Take a ball of ice,
the sort found in cocktails
clinking against the glass.

Scoop one out,
hold it between
your forefinger and thumb.

Hold it up.
Yes it is dripping.
It's meant to.

That's the world melting.

A Fuchsia Flowers in Winter

Melancholy of bell-like
flowers – mauve-red pink
weeping unreservedly –

draws me towards
this snowblink vision,
petals sore with tears,

branches broken, frostbitten,
earth's deep sadness
spelt in snow.

The Sun

hangs over London, as if she's stalking me.
The lawn has burnt patches, like a blister
which won't heal. Weather forecasters are excited,

maybe they're lying. In the Arctic, a mammoth
iceberg hunches its shoulders, splits, topples over.
The cast-off, a small country, floats towards

the warmth, its watery cargo melting.
In Zermatt there's been no January snow.
Spoilt bankers and their hedge-fund cousins

feel let down. They don't know what it's like
to be let down. They will soon learn.
Two months pass and so does the panic.

Life returns: a skinny latte for her, a double
espresso and chocolate croissant for me.
For the second year, infernos on the moors flare up.

Twenty-foot flames lap the air. Fires sprint all over.
Everyone is playing with water. Want to join in?
No I don't think so, they wouldn't want me anyway.

The ground steams. Carbon from peat poisons
the sky. Again, fires take two months to drown.
Have you ever seen a dust bowl? Do you want to?

There may be one blowing our way. East Anglia
is a good candidate. No, you can't buy tickets.
Newspapers stop scare stories, but John Lewis

have just made a vast order for hand-held fans.
The sun is still wearing her *I told you so* smile
as she glugs a glass of dry white.

Flooded McDonald's
(*In response to the film by Superflex*)

McDonald's is drowning, not globally yet, just
a small branch in a nowhere coastal town, USA.

The sea roars along Main Street, through
the restaurant's open doors, over the tables,

chairs, and counter. Customers rushing into the street
are swept away. Water pressure is so strong it slams

the fridge door on the manager – he's been checking
supplies. He fumbles for his mobile to say goodbye,

drops it, sees the light fade as it sinks to the floor.
The fryer is swallowed. Chips, a pile of plastic cups,

a till, all float then submerge. Bins are flooded,
rubbish bobs in the street. The body of an elderly

man trapped in the toilet, floats to the surface
then sweeps through the main doors. The water rises,

creeps up the shop front to the defiant restaurant sign.
Its lights flicker, splutter, extinguish. The sea still roars.

Tonight, on the evening news in London, a tweet
from Trump refers to a one-off, very, very rare incident.

Heat Wave

DAY 10
"Two minutes longer," the weatherman said,
daylight had been two minutes longer.
Then he said June sun was very strong.
Where's the science, I thought?
Had he been told any?

Sky was a brilliant blue, gleamed
its blistered smile, air was a dry breath.

Weatherman hurried off to the Serpentine,
to row in the cool of the lake. Parks were full;
stripped workers simmered on the grass.
Skin reddened. A swan's neck flopped
into the water.

Headlines caught the news late, or dropped it.
I hunted for Evian, but any brand would do.
Too late. At Asda, daylight stood on empty shelves.

DAY 19

Heat grew. I noticed white vapour wriggle
through the air. The parks boiled. The beach at Brighton
had no spare deck chairs. A battalion of gulls
bobbed in the sea. Sun block was getting low.

The Royal Marsden's skin man broke first,
on a Panorama special, talked of covering up,
long sleeves, veils. Where do I buy a veil?
He spoke like an uncle, in plain weather, big numbers,
said something weird,
that weather would improve.
He knew, wasn't telling.

Cold air units, electric fans became daily bread. Lorries
on delivery to Argos were mobbed.
Ice cream was treasure. I found two cases of Evian,
padlocked the shed.

Air was blowing on a thirsty setting,
the sun was growing colour,
became the darkest shade of orange.

DAY 23
I thought a lot, imagined two weeks ahead,
then a month, shivered with the heat of it.
Glad I had no children.

I phoned Kate. Reception was breaking up.
She cried.
"But it's just sun," she said.

Pigeons hopped on hot pavements, kept to shade
of thinning trees.
News was anorexic,
still lacked real science.
I checked the lock on the shed.

DAY 40
Someone said earth's spin had slowed, minutely,
would correct. Someone else said that couldn't happen.
Everyone's being awfully clever
but still no expert opinions broadcast.

Clouds were now thin sheets, worn nylon.
Sun's rays pelted the reservoirs, gulped my pond.
Grass was yellow, died back.
Heat went up another two notches on the hair dryer.
My canary died. I'd forgotten fresh water.
A squirrel fell from my tree.

DAY 55

I phoned BA, hung on, tortured by four hours
of muzak, menus, unhelpful advice,
should have phoned Qantas.
I booked two to the other side. Transferred savings,
cooling as they whizzed: London to Sydney into
Australian dollars. I'd bought a few months.
Felt… can't explain.

That evening Kate kissed me, her mouth clinging
to mine. Her breath sizzled, her skin was scorched
and outside sister sun blazed.
I stroked her neck, shoulders, arms,
kissed her eyes.
She broke away.

There are degrees of love, aren't there?
You can't argue with climate,
persuade what is there to shine.
She left me.

DAY 60
Off to Heathrow, Check In, then Passport Control.
We all gulp the air conditioning, drink it down.
Hazy heat has a troubled stare.
Police usher us to the plane, two hundred metres
from the terminal. A queue-jumper is bundled to the back.

I spot a fox giddy with heat, paws stuck to tarmac,
his *what's happening* eyes are blurred,
tail a shadow. I hope we're allowed to fly.

On board we wait and wait.
A stewardess has a smile Sellotaped to her mouth.
Her eyes are empty.

Some joker wants a poem for his time capsule.

Inspiration
Or, Where I Find My Ideas

When I left school in 1965, the Head Master sent me John Betjeman's Collected Poems. I don't know why, I can't recall that I particularly deserved it. Two years later I sent him a poem. This was prompted by a newspaper item which concerned what I thought was an injustice and an act of snobbery. It was about someone who was unable to achieve membership of a golf club, where my Head Master was a member. The poem had found me.

Years later around 1994, when I seriously took up poetry, I joined the inspirational Dinah Livingstone's poetry workshop, at the Working Men's College in London. I recall bringing an elegy. Again the poem had found me, I had to write it. We always discussed a poem introduced by Dinah. On one occasion, 'Prayer', a sonnet by Carol Ann Duffy was presented. It affected me, and I wrote my own sonnet, 'Painful Prayer', in response.

At the newly founded Poetry School on Saturdays, led by the remarkable duo of Mimi Khalvati and Jane Duran, I was also introduced to Duffy's 'Warming Her Pearls'. I then wrote a poem called 'Her Pearls'. We weren't being asked to respond, but often I couldn't resist.

I also attended the City Lit where the late Julia Casterton taught poetry. One day, she tentatively explained her illness and suggested we all write a poem about blood. This would not normally have been a subject to inspire me. However, men and women alike all adored Julia. It was because of this affection that the emotional impulse took over and most of us wrote the poem.

These anecdotes stem from my early years of writing. Gradually, I was beginning to understand where poems came from. Initially, I was mainly mining experience. However, after a visit to the north Norfolk coast, I realized it was possible to have feelings for the natural world. The poems poured out. It hadn't occurred to me that a London boy could be so influenced.

In 2010 I attended *Acumen*'s 25th anniversary which also celebrated the magazine's 60th issue. It was held at Bonhams in New Bond Street and was a jolly occasion. Wine was everywhere. I had never attended a poetry event where wine was constantly offered and nearing the end I had to sit down.

That event inspired a poem called 'Waiting for the Wine'. It led to the birth of the fictional poet George Meadows. Poems about his blundering, eccentric life cascaded towards me. There were so many arriving that I had to take my notebook to bed. In the space between when I shut my eyes and fell to sleep, I was writing the titles to poems, so I wouldn't forget them by the morning. The plan worked well and subsequently I was able to write about seventy poems. My now ex-wife had to get used to me continually turning on the bedside light. Actually, she was very good about it!

So where else do poems come from? I read that Michael Longley said if he knew, he'd go there. George Meadows says he gets his ideas from a charity shop, they're usually the cheapest and he's helping good causes at the same time. He says The British Heart Foundation and Age UK are particularly good.

For me it's mostly about reading, being receptive, patient and experienced enough to know which random thoughts and instincts can best be developed in a truthful way. Writing in other voices, especially flowers and animals has also been helpful in growing themes and ideas.

However, I've learnt that my poems don't always do as they're told. They often misbehave. When that happens I put them aside, let the little darlings have a rest or even a sleep; this can be for few days, weeks, or even years. It's surprising how time helps. If I wake them with a kiss, they are usually pleased to see me.

*

The following poem was inspired by teaching poetry to my thirteen-year-old grandson. My daughter had asked if I'd like to do this once a week, during the summer holidays. I asked him if he liked sausages. I couldn't resist joining in.

In Praise of Sausages
(*For Arthur*)

Dear sausages, yes you lounging on a bed
of mash, togged up in a brown gravy suit.
Please wave me a smile of apple and chives
with caress of petit pois on the side.

Now I'll ask for onion rings, fried
golden bangles, a crisp explosion of bite
peppered with chilli flakes, and to cleanse
my mouth, a quick milkshake kiss at midnight.

But back to sausages, mash, peas and onions –
glistening, gorgeously mushy. You are
my king of meals, a sexy knee, some hanky
panky, a latin verb, chanting:

Amo amas amat, I love you dear porky.

About the Author

Peter Phillips is a London poet.

His previous collections are:

Four Poems from Saying It With Flowers
(pamphlet), 2016, Hearing Eye

Oscar and I, 2013, Ward Wood Publishing

No School Tie, 2011, Ward Wood Publishing

Wide Skies, Salt and Best Bitter, 2005, Hearing Eye

Looking for You, 2001, Hearing Eye

Frayed at the Edges, (pamphlet), 1997, Hearing Eye

For more about this author online, see his pages on the *poetry pf* website www.poetrypf.co.uk
and on wardwoodpublishing.co.uk